Cliff

D0628735

Much Ado About Nothing

By Richard O. Peterson, Ph.D.

IN THIS BOOK

- *Discover the plot, significant themes, and main characters of* Much Ado About Nothing

- *Prepare for classroom discussion, essays, and tests*

- *Gain an understanding of how the Kenneth Branagh film of* Much Ado About Nothing *differs from the play*

- *Reinforce what you learn with CliffsNotes Review*

- *Find more information on Shakespeare and Much Ado About Nothing in CliffsNotes Resource Center and online at* www.cliffsnotes.com

Houghton Mifflin Harcourt
Boston New York

Publisher's Acknowledgments
Acquisitions Editor:
  Greg Tubach

Project Editor:
  Elizabeth Netedu Kuball

CliffsNotes™ *Much Ado About Nothing*
Published by:
Houghton Mifflin Harcourt

Copyright © 2014 Houghton Mifflin Harcourt
ISBN: 0-7645-8505-3
Printed in the United States of America
DOH 15 14 13 12 11 10 9 8
1O/ST/QZ/QT/IN
4500477968

For information about permission to reproduce selections from this book, write to Permissions, Houghton Mifflin Harcourt Publishing Company, 215 Park Avenue South, New York, New York 10003.

www.hmhco.com

CONTENTS

MUCH ADO ABOUT NOTHING

Notes

LIFE AND BACKGROUND OF THE AUTHOR

Many books have assembled facts, reasonable suppositions, traditions, and speculations concerning the life and career of William Shakespeare. Taken as a whole, these materials give a rather comprehensive picture of England's foremost dramatic poet. Tradition and sober supposition are not necessarily false because they lack proved bases for their existence. Persons interested in Shakespeare should, however, make a distinction between the facts of Shakespeare's life and what we believe to be true about him.

From one point of view, modern scholars are fortunate to know as much as they do about a man of middle-class origin who left a small country town and embarked on a professional career in sixteenth-century London. From another point of view, they know surprisingly little about the writer who has continued to influence the English language and its drama and poetry for more than 300 years. Sparse and scattered as these facts of his life are, they are sufficient to prove that a man from Stratford by the name of William Shakespeare wrote the major portion of the 37 plays that scholars ascribe to him. The concise review that follows concerns itself with some of these records, which are primarily important because they prove the existence of a William Shakespeare in Stratford and in London during this period.

No one knows the exact date of William Shakespeare's birth. His baptism occurred on Wednesday, April 26, 1564. His father was John Shakespeare, tanner, glover, dealer in grain, and town official of Stratford; his mother, Mary, was the daughter of Robert Arden, a prosperous gentleman-farmer. The Shakespeares lived on Henley Street in Stratford, located about 100 miles northwest of London.

Under a bond dated November 28, 1582, William Shakespeare and Anne Hathaway entered into a marriage contract. The baptism of their eldest child, Susanna, took place in Stratford in May 1583. One year and nine months later, their twins, Hamnet and Judith, were christened in the same church. William and Anne named them for the poet's friends, Hamnet and Judith Sadler.

Early in 1596, William Shakespeare, in his father's name, applied to the College of Heralds for a coat of arms. Although positive proof is lacking, there is reason to believe that the Heralds granted this request, for in 1599, Shakespeare made application for the right to quarter his coat of arms with that of his mother. Entitled to her father's coat of arms, Mary had lost this privilege when she married John Shakespeare before he held the official status of gentleman.

In May 1597, Shakespeare purchased New Place, the outstanding residential property in Stratford at that time. Since John Shakespeare had suffered financial reverses prior to this date, William must have achieved success for himself.

Court records show that in 1601–1602, William Shakespeare began rooming in the household of Christopher Mountjoy in London. Subsequent disputes over the wedding settlement and agreement between Mountjoy and his son-in-law, Stephen Belott, led to a series of legal actions, and in 1612, the court scribe recorded Shakespeare's deposition of testimony relating to the case.

In July 1605, William Shakespeare paid 440 pounds for the lease of a large portion of the tithes on certain real estate in and near Stratford, an arrangement whereby Shakespeare purchased half the annual tithes, or taxes, on certain agricultural products from parcels of land in and near Stratford. In addition to receiving approximately ten percent income on his investment, he almost doubled his capital. This investment was possibly the most important and successful one of his lifetime, and it paid a steady income for many years.

Shakespeare is next mentioned when John Combe, a resident of Stratford, died on July 12, 1614. To his friend, Combe bequeathed the sum of five pounds.

On March 25, 1616, William Shakespeare revised his last will and testament. He died on April 23 of the same year. His body lies within the chancel and before the altar of the Holy Trinity Church, located in Stratford. A rather wry inscription is carved upon his tombstone:

Good Friend, for Jesus' sake, forbear
To dig the dust enclosed here;
Blest be the man that spares these bones
And curst be he who moves my bones.

The last direct descendant of William Shakespeare was his granddaughter, Elizabeth Hall, who died in 1670.

These are the most outstanding facts about Shakespeare the man, as apart from those about the dramatist and poet. Such pieces of information, scattered from 1564 through 1616, declare the existence of such a person, not as a writer or an actor, but as a private citizen. Although some people doubt the existence of one poet and playwright known as William Shakespeare and believe his plays were written by a *group* of men, it is illogical to think that anyone would or could have fabricated these details for the purpose of deceiving later generations.

In similar fashion, the evidence establishing William Shakespeare as the foremost playwright of his day is positive and persuasive. Robert Greene's *Groatsworth of Wit, Bought with a Million of Repentance,* in which he attacked Shakespeare, a mere actor, for presuming to write plays in competition with Greene and his fellow playwrights, was entered in the Stationers' Register on September 20, 1592. In 1594, Shakespeare acted before Queen Elizabeth, and in 1594–1595, his name appeared as one of the shareholders of the Lord Chamberlain's Company. Francis Meres in his *Palladis Tamia* (1598) called Shakespeare "mellifluous and hony-tongued" and compared his comedies and tragedies with those of Plautus and Seneca in excellence.

Shakespeare's continued association with Burbage's company is equally definite. His name appears as one of the owners of London's Globe theater in 1599. On May 19, 1603, he and his fellow actors received a patent from James I designating them as the King's Men and making them Grooms of the Chamber. Late in 1608 or early in 1609, Shakespeare and his colleagues purchased the Blackfriars Theatre and began using it as their winter location when weather made production at the Globe inconvenient.

Other specific allusions to Shakespeare, to his acting, and to his writing, occur in numerous places. Put together, they form irrefutable testimony that William Shakespeare of Stratford and London was the leader among Elizabethan playwrights.

One of the most impressive of all proofs of Shakespeare's authorship of his plays is the First Folio of 1623, with the dedicatory verse that appeared in it. John Heminge and Henry Condell, members of Shakespeare's own acting company, stated that they collected and issued the plays as a memorial to their fellow actor. Many contemporary poets contributed eulogies to Shakespeare; one of the best-known of these poems is by Ben Jonson, a fellow actor and, later, a friendly rival. Jonson also criticized Shakespeare's dramatic work in *Timber: or, Discoveries* (1640).

Certainly there are many things about Shakespeare's genius and career that the most diligent scholars do not know and cannot explain, but the facts that do exist are sufficient to establish Shakespeare's identity as a man and his authorship of the 37 plays that reputable critics acknowledge to be his. Someone obviously wrote these dramatic masterpieces, and Shakespeare remains the only candidate worthy of serious consideration.

INTRODUCTION TO THE PLAY

Much Ado About Nothing is one of Shakespeare's most frequently performed comedies. Probably written in the latter part of 1598, it was performed soon afterward by the Lord Chamberlain's Men, the theatrical company in which William Shakespeare had a business interest separate from his duties as actor and playwright.

Much Ado is apparently based on a story in a collection of stories by Italian writer Matteo Bandello, originally published in 1554 and translated into English in 1582. Some plot elements and characters may have been inspired by a lengthy Italian poem, *Orlando Furioso* by Ludovico Aristo, originally published in 1532 and translated into English in 1591.

The broad comedy in *Much Ado* has early twentieth-century parallels in the romantic "screwball" comedies of the 1930s — for example, *It Happened One Night* with Clark Gable and Claudette Colbert, *Ninotchka* with Greta Garbo and Melvin Douglas, and *The*

Awful Truth with Cary Grant and Irene Dunne. The scenes with Dogberry and his men find ready counterparts in early movies featuring the Keystone Kops and the Marx Brothers.

If *Much Ado* were only a play depicting its characters as products of their circumstances and the situations they encounter, the play would seem quite shallow and would probably not be popular today. However, most of the complications and problems are resolved through psychological growth in several characters rather than merely through changes in circumstances (see the Character Analyses later in this study guide).

Most Shakespeare authorities agree that the word "nothing" in the play's title is purposely ambiguous. In Elizabethan times, "nothing" was pronounced much like "noting," which means not only taking note or observing, but also overhearing or intentionally eavesdropping — actions around which the plot turns and twists (see the essay "About 'Nothing'" later in this study guide).

A BRIEF SYNOPSIS

The action of *Much Ado About Nothing* occurs during several days of a visit by Don Pedro, Prince of Aragon, and his followers at the large estate of Leonato, Governor of Messina. Don Pedro has been victorious in a small war against his own half-brother, Don John, who has now (reluctantly) joined him.

From the beginning to the end of the play, two love stories are intertwined. One story follows the formal, romantic relationship between Leonato's daughter, Hero (a young woman), and Claudio (a young officer): Claudio realizes, after returning from war, that he is deeply in love with Hero and wants to ask her father for permission to marry her. His commander, Don Pedro, helps Claudio propose marriage, with some momentary confusion about who the suitor is — Don Pedro or Claudio.

The other couple, Beatrice (Hero's cousin) and Benedick (another officer), work hard to give the impression that neither is the least bit interested in the other, still smarting over bad experiences in earlier encounters with one another. From the beginning of the play, Beatrice and Benedick tease and insult one another mercilessly and repeatedly deny that they will ever marry anyone, let alone marry one another. However, the audience can tell almost immediately that they don't entirely believe their own disclaimers. Their friends arrange for them to overhear conversations revealing how much each is loved by the other.

Meanwhile, the defeated Don John, a self-proclaimed villain, is eager to carry out serious mischief against his brother and Claudio, who helped defeat him. One of John's men enacts a scene at Hero's window in which a woman who appears to be Hero succumbs to the amorous attentions of a man other than Claudio. John further arranges for Claudio and Don Pedro to observe this scene. As a result of seeing this apparent deception, Claudio angrily denounces Hero during their wedding ceremony and, with Don Pedro, storms off as the deceived husband-to-be. The friar performing the ceremony comforts Hero, her father, and the other couple (Benedick and Beatrice), and arranges for Hero to be hidden as though dead, until Claudio regains his senses. Beatrice's defense of Hero after her denouncement unites Beatrice and Benedick in the cause of Hero's revenge, and they declare their love for one another.

In the meantime, Dogberry (a comically bumbling constable) and his men on night watch stumble on the conspiracy against Don Pedro and arrest John's men, who confess their guilt under questioning.

Soon Claudio is forced to admit his error in thinking that Hero would deceive him and, believing her dead, mourns for her and agrees to marry one of Hero's cousins. The cousin turns out to be a disguised and forgiving Hero. Beatrice and Benedick are also to be married. Don John tries to run off but is recaptured.

LIST OF CHARACTERS

LEONATO'S HOUSEHOLD

Leonato

Governor of Messina, a city in Renaissance Italy. Most of the play takes place in and around Leonato's home and estate. He is father to Hero, uncle and guardian to Beatrice, and host to Don Pedro and his entourage. Friendly and unsophisticated, influenced by appearances and opinions of others, Leonato is a unifying figure, linking the play's plot lines to one another from first scene to last.

Hero

Daughter of Leonato and Claudio's intended wife-to-be. Quiet, traditional, obedient, and naive, she becomes the unwitting victim of Don John's plot to cause mischief for Don Pedro and Claudio. Her loyalties shift easily: first willing to accept Don Pedro's apparent proposal, then readily shifting to Claudio. Later, even after her humiliation by him, she is quite prepared to marry a repentant Claudio.

Beatrice

Orphaned niece of Leonato, raised in his household as a second daughter. Strong-willed, opinionated, and outspoken, she has been emotionally wounded by Benedick in earlier encounters and has built a defense system against him with sarcasm, wit, disparagement, and apparent indifference. She is protective of Hero, her cousin.

Antonio

Brother of Leonato and a member of his household.

Margaret

One of two gentlewomen (maidservants) to Hero. Margaret's remarks often include sexual innuendoes. She is innocently misled by Borachio into the plot to deceive Claudio and Don Pedro.

Ursula

The second of Hero's maidservants. Ursula plays a small role in deceiving Beatrice about Benedick's love.

Friar Francis

The good friar who is to perform the marriage of Hero and Claudio. Friar Francis proposes the scheme to hide Hero after her denunciation, pretending she is dead.

DON PEDRO'S COMPANY

Don Pedro

A prince of Aragon (spelled Arragon in some editions), a region of northeast Spain (which helps explain why he carries the Spanish title of respect, Don). Like Leonato, Don Pedro is a linking character, playing key roles first in the wooing of Hero for Claudio, then in the deceptions of both Beatrice and Benedick, and finally as an unwitting eyewitness to Don John's staging of Hero's unfaithfulness. He apparently likes to control events around him but in fact becomes a victim of them and seems the lesser for being deceived.

Claudio

A young count from the city of Florence (he has an uncle in Messina) who is a companion to Don Pedro and has played a heroic part in the fight against Don John. Having admired Hero before going off to war, on his return he is much taken with her — and perhaps with her future inheritance. He seems immature and easily misled by the suggestions and actions of others, including Don Pedro, Don John, and Leonato. His affections are mercurial — back and forth between infatuation and rejection. He is committed to a personal code of ethics that prevents him from accepting a "tarnished" bride.

Benedick

Another soldier in Don Pedro's company, not a count like Claudio, but referred to respectfully as "signor." Benedick enjoyed the company of Beatrice at some earlier time but went away without any commitment causing her to harden her attitudes about men and marriage — an appropriate match for Benedick's own attitudes about women and marriage. He is witty and often sarcastic, independent in spirit, loyal to friends — and not really the misogynist (woman hater) he appears to be. He is quite ready to believe that Beatrice loves him and is not afraid of changing his mind, even publicly.

Don John

Brother to Don Pedro. Because he was born outside of marriage, he has no official claim to any of his family's wealth or position. He tried to overthrow his brother in battle but lost. Now his brother's generosity in accepting him as part of his company grates on Don John's unaccommodating personality, and he longs to get back at his brother.

Borachio

One of Don John's personal followers. Borachio has had a personal relationship with Margaret one of Hero's attendants. He uses this relationship for Don John s mischief and his own personal profit by devising the deceptive "window scene." His later repentance seems to stem at least partly from a recognition that the deception went too far.

Conrade (spelled Conrad in some editions)

Another of Don John's personal followers.

Balthasar

A musician in Don Pedro's company.

MESSINA'S CONSTABLES

Dogberry

The constable of Messina, in charge of the night watch — a wonderfully comic figure. Dogberry may be a man of "low station" and rough habits, especially as demonstrated in his garbled speech, but his pride and his wit suggest that some of his actions and expressions may be intentionally ambiguous and provocative.

Verges

The deputy constable ("headborough") of Messina and Dogberry's constant companion.

George Seacoal and Other Watchmen

The words and actions of the watchmen make them seem more alert and intelligent than Dogberry and Verges. After all, they overhear Don John's plot with Borachio, report the misdeed, and provide testimony that convicts Borachio and ultimately Don John.

Sexton

A public official who records the testimony in a trial.

CRITICAL COMMENTARIES

ACT I — SCENE 1

Summary

A messenger delivers a letter to Leonato, governor of Messina, announcing that Don Pedro, Prince of Aragon, will arrive shortly. Don Pedro and his followers have emerged victorious and almost unscathed after halting a rebellion by his own brother, Don John. The messenger reports that Claudio, a young lord of Florence, has carried himself especially well and is much honored by Don Pedro. Leonato's niece Beatrice asks the messenger about the fate of another of Don Pedro's men: Benedick of Padua. Apparently, she does not think well of him, as indicated by her scathing remarks about him. The messenger reports that Benedick also acquitted himself well in the battle and is now a companion of Claudio's.

Don Pedro soon arrives with Claudio and Benedick, as well as Don John and other soldiers. Leonato graciously receives the visitors and invites them to stay for at least a month.

Left to themselves, Beatrice and Benedick exchange taunts and insults, symptomatic of their "merry war."

Later, alone with Benedick, Claudio confides that he wants to marry Hero, Leonato's daughter. He ignores Benedick's heckling about marriage and his disparagement of Hero. Don Pedro reenters and is told about Claudio's intent to seek Hero for his wife. Don Pedro encourages Claudio and promises to approach Hero and her father on Claudio's behalf during the evening's masked celebrations.

Commentary

The battle between the forces of Don Pedro and his rebellious brother Don John is alluded to quite briefly in references to the few casualties suffered and the valor of both Claudio and Benedick. The audience gets a first clue about the discord between Don John and Don Pedro when the stage direction refers to "Don John the Bastard," and a second clue when Leonato refers to John as being "reconciled to the Prince your brother." Not until Act I, Scene 3, does the audience learn how his defeat and his submissive position in his brother's circle humiliates Don John and electrifies his desire to create trouble in the household, especially for Claudio, who was instrumental in his defeat.

In this first scene, all four "romantic" young people who will remain at the center of the play's action are introduced:

Hero represents a young woman in tune with the traditions of the time — seen but seldom heard, deferential to her father, awaiting an appropriate suitor to take formal steps to court her. In keeping with her modest demeanor, Hero has only one brief line during this scene, but she is the subject of conversation as soon as she leaves the stage.

By contrast, *Beatrice* tends to take charge of every conversation, not reluctant to state her own views on a subject regardless of whom she addresses. Her wit and sarcasm are wasted on the messenger, who doesn't know what to make of her. Her uncle, Leonato, acknowledges her ongoing "merry war" with Benedick. Finally, she engages Benedick himself, who can give back as good as he gets.

Before he appears, *Claudio* is reported to be much honored by his commanding officer, Don Pedro. Like Hero, he is quiet when Don Pedro and his men are welcomed by Leonato. But when everyone leaves, Claudio immediately begins talking about his love for Hero in a very traditional manner, prompting Benedick to rant against women in general and Hero in particular. Claudio readily accepts Don Pedro's offer to speak both to Hero and to her father for him. During this planning, Claudio determines that Hero is Leonato's only heir.

Benedick too is mentioned before he appears, but only by Beatrice, who is clearly bitter toward him, apparently as the result of previous experience with him. In his battle of words with Beatrice, Benedick puts up a noble fight, finally putting her on the defensive, but while Benedick has the last word this time, Beatrice ends the conversation with an aside, spoken for the benefit of the audience, revealing that she and Benedick have known each other personally in the past and that this war of words is not something new. Regarding his attitudes about women, Benedick admits that he is a "professed tyrant to their sex."

This one scene literally sets the stage for all the main events to follow: the courtship and anticipated marriage of Hero and Claudio, the thorny relationship between Beatrice and Benedick, and the disruptive mischief of Don John.

The first instance of wordplay on "noting/nothing" (see the essay, "About 'Nothing'") appears in this scene:

Claudio: Benedick, didst thou note the daughter of Signor Leonato?
Benedick: I noted her not, but I looked on her.

This dialogue introduces two meanings of the word "note": observe and study.

The groundwork for the play's first deception is soon laid: Not only will Don Pedro speak to Hero on Claudio's behalf, but he will be wearing a mask and pretending to be Claudio.

The next two scenes will reveal that the conversation between Claudio and Don Pedro has been overheard ("noted") by at least two others: by Antonio's "man" and by Borachio, one of Don John's followers. The conversation is misunderstood by Antonio's man, leading to some confusion, but correctly reported by Borachio to Don John, leading to a first deception to be set up by Don John.

ACT I — SCENE 2

Summary

In this very short scene, Antonio erroneously reports to his brother Leonato that Don Pedro is in love with Hero and will approach both her and Leonato at the coming dance. Leonato asks Antonio to tell Hero about it.

Commentary

Here is the result of the first incident of overhearing or *noting*. Antonio's man who overheard the final conversation of the first scene — between Don Pedro and Claudio — did not understand that Don Pedro would be speaking to Hero and her father on behalf of Claudio rather than for himself. Thus, the stage is set for a misunderstanding: Don Pedro's masked wooing of Hero is likely to be misinterpreted by Hero because Antonio will have told her that Don Pedro desires her for himself.

Borachio overheard the same conversation and will report it to his master, Don John, in the next scene.

Although the first line of this scene refers to Antonio's son, Hero is later declared to be the sole heir of both Antonio and Leonato (Act V, Scene 1). The present version of the play is the product of several revisions by Shakespeare as well as by his first editors and publishers. In one version, Antonio's son appeared in this scene with a musician. He was edited out of the scene but is still referred to incidentally here, although later he doesn't exist at all.

ACT I — SCENE 3

Summary

Don John complains to his companion Conrade (Conrad in some editions) about his position in life: He is Don Pedro's bastard brother, recently defeated, without pretenses or mannerly habits, facing his dishonorable status daily while enduring his brother's hospitality. All in all, he displays a generally disagreeable attitude and seems determined to make the most of it. His second companion, Borachio, enters to report having overheard (*noted*) the conversation between Don Pedro and Claudio wherein "the Prince should woo Hero for himself and, having obtained her, give her to Count Claudio."

Don John immediately sees this plan as an opportunity to do mischief both to Claudio — honored for his actions against Don John — and to Don Pedro. Don John and his men head out for the celebratory supper, Don John expressing regret that the cook is not on his side and ready to dispatch the assembled household and guests with poison.

Commentary

Although the audience was introduced to an apparently submissive Don John in Scene 1, in this scene in no way is he subdued. In fact, he feels compelled to create trouble for the two men who are responsible for his recent defeat — Don Pedro and Claudio. When Borachio reports having hidden behind a tapestry to overhear the conversation about Claudio's intentions toward Hero, Don John is cheered by the idea that he can use this situation as "food to my displeasure."

This scene includes the second reported incident of overhearing/noting. Borachio has eavesdropped on the same conversation that someone reported incorrectly to Antonio — but Borachio gets it right.

The character developed as Don John is sometimes criticized because he does not have any real motive for disrupting the marriage of Hero and Claudio. Rather, this scene provides a clear motive for getting back at Claudio:

> That young start-up [upstart] hath all the glory of my overthrow. If I can cross him any way, I bless myself every way.

Because Don Pedro is supportive of Claudio, any action against Claudio will also be an insult to his brother — his ultimate target for trouble. The audience does not have to assume any innate or unexplainable streak of evil in Don John. The man does, however, seem to relish his villainy.

ACT II — SCENE 1

Summary

The celebration and dance scene includes several short encounters among many of the characters. Most participants are masked, adding to the confusion.

First, Leonato, Antonio, Hero, and Beatrice appear, commenting on Don John's sad and sour appearance. Beatrice uses the occasion as another opportunity to berate Benedick. Leonato and Antonio warn her she is heading for spinsterhood if she continues her attitudes about Benedick in particular and about men and marriage in general. As usual, Hero says very little. To Beatrice's amusement, Hero is cautioned by both her uncle and her father to be attentive and receptive to Don Pedro when he approaches her this evening. (They believe he is courting her for himself.) As guests arrive, Leonato signals everyone to get masks and to mix with the guests. Soon everyone except for Don John and Borachio is masked.

With sweet words, Don Pedro asks Hero to dance ("walk a bout") with him. Then the musician Balthasar and Margaret are overheard in a flirtatious exchange, followed by a similar flirtation by Antonio with Ursula. When the masked Beatrice and Benedick have a brief encounter, she does not seem to know him with his mask and tells this stranger how upset she is with Benedick.

Borachio points out the masked Claudio to Don John. Pretending that Claudio is Benedick, Don John tells him that Don Pedro has sworn his affection for Hero and swears to marry her. He asks Claudio-as-Benedick to talk Don Pedro out of marriage since Hero is "no equal for his birth." Don John and Borachio leave Claudio lamenting the deception by his Prince. Benedick appears and tries to joke about Claudio's apparent loss of Hero, but Claudio walks away in distress.

Don Pedro appears, and Benedick tells him of Claudio's heartache at the prince's winning of Hero. Surprised, Don Pedro says he has always intended to court Hero only for Claudio. When Beatrice appears with Claudio, Benedick hurriedly leaves.

Claudio returns and Don Pedro makes it clear to him that, just as planned, he has spoken to Hero only for Claudio. He signals for

Leonato and Hero to join them. Hero is shy when Claudio expresses his renewed joy, and Beatrice chides her. When Don Pedro jokes with Beatrice about finding her a husband now, even himself, Beatrice quickly leaves. After a date is set for the wedding of Claudio and Hero, Don Pedro proposes a scheme to bring Beatrice and Benedick together. Leonato, Claudio, and Hero all agree to help in the plan.

Commentary

This long scene may be confusing, because events significant to the forward movement of the story are intermixed with insignificant events. Furthermore everyone except the villains — Don John and his cohorts — are masked. To make the scene even more confusing, two unrelated plots are hatched — Don John's first plot and Don Pedro's plot for bringing Beatrice and Benedick together. And the scene has many sub-scenes: the opening conversation about Don John and about Beatrice's future; the dance that includes several short conversations; the deception of Claudio by Don John; the clarification by Don Pedro; the blessing of Claudio and Hero for their marriage; and finally Don Pedro's plot for Beatrice and Benedick.

When the dancing starts, it may help readers to imagine couples moving in a large circle around the stage, pausing briefly so the audience overhears parts of their conversations: Don Pedro and Hero, Balthasar and Margaret, Antonio and Ursula, and Beatrice and Benedick. The brief appearances of these characters reveal much about their personalities:

Leonato and his family perceive a dark side to Don John;

Claudio is immature and quite suggestible and his emotions are very fragile — important to keep in mind for later;

Hero continues to be submissive and shy;

Beatrice, who recognizes her own contrariness and directness and their effects on others, especially men, has been hurt by Benedick sometime in the past;

Benedick is vulnerable to Beatrice's barbs (by the end of the scene, Benedick is at his most exasperated with Beatrice's insults, referring to her as a Harpy and as Lady

Tongue; he asks Don Pedro to send him on any errand, no matter how ridiculous, just to get him away from Beatrice);

Don Pedro likes to play the role of a prince, manipulating the lives of others: his nearly misfired wooing of Hero for Claudio; his lighthearted offer of himself as a husband to Beatrice, fully aware she would not accept him; his scheme to bring Beatrice and Benedick together;

Margaret is a flirt; and

Ursula is sensitive to the feelings of others (realizing Antonio is offended by her mild taunts of him).

ACT II — SCENE 2

Summary

Don John is disappointed that his first attempt to sabotage Claudio and Don Pedro did not work: Claudio and Hero are still to be married. Borachio assures him he can disrupt the wedding with Don John's help. He suggests that Don John tell Claudio and Don Pedro that Hero is unfaithful. To counter their expected disbelief, Don John will lead them to a place below Hero's window on the night before the wedding. Then Borachio and his friend Margaret will appear at the window, making it look like Hero and another man are in an embrace. Borachio points out that the plot will have a fourfold impact: "to misuse the Prince, to vex Claudio, to undo Hero and kill Leonato." Don John promises to reward Borachio generously for his efforts if the plan works.

Commentary

The audience has to imagine some of the unreported details of Borachio's plot. Although we accept that Borachio will be able to entice Margaret (his intimate friend for a year) to Hero's room and its window, how he will persuade her to act the role of Hero is unclear. Perhaps he will talk her into pretending that they are the happy couple about to be married. Margaret frequently uses words and ideas with sexual overtones, so enticing her into the window scene may not be difficult. Don John will tell the prince and Claudio that Hero loves Borachio, probably so that when they see him in the window, they will recognize him. Presumably, Margaret will be made to resemble Hero, at least at a distance.

ACT II — SCENE 3

Summary

Alone, Benedick talks to himself about how Claudio has changed since his engagement to Hero. Benedick has lost a good friend since Claudio now thinks of nothing but Hero and their approaching wedding. He ponders what perfect combination of qualities a woman must possess before he himself would marry her.

When Benedick hears Claudio, Leonato, and Don Pedro approaching, he hides in the arbor to eavesdrop/note what they say.

Don Pedro and the others know that Benedick has hidden himself within the sound of their voices. Don Pedro asks the musician Balthasar to sing for them, and he sings a song that begins, "*Sigh no more, ladies, sigh no more. Men were deceivers ever.*"

After the singer leaves, Don Pedro, Claudio, and Leonato converse loudly about how much Beatrice really loves Benedick in spite of the way she treats him. She will not show affection toward him for fear that she will be rejected. They agree not to speak of it to Benedick for now, and they leave.

Benedick can scarcely believe what he has heard, but because Leonato was part of the group, he does not think it can be a joke. He admits that he did not plan to marry and has been contemptuous of marriage, but maybe he can change for the sake of Beatrice. In fact, he suddenly realizes she has all those qualities he was enumerating earlier.

Beatrice reluctantly approaches Benedick to call him for dinner. When he tries to speak kindly to her, she replies unkindly and leaves. He tries to read love into her words and reaffirms to himself that he must try to love her.

Commentary

This scene is the first of two contrived overhearing/noting scenes in Don Pedro's plan to bring Beatrice and Benedick together. Benedick does not perceive that they have set him up; instead, he eavesdrops/notes the contrived conversation about

Beatrice and her love for him and believes it all. The next scene — Act III, Scene 1 — is a parallel scene in which Beatrice over-hears/notes a conversation about Benedick's love for her.

Benedick is first suspicious that this is a "gull" — a hoax cooked up by his friends — but Leonato, "the white-bearded fellow speaks it: knavery cannot sure hide himself in such reverence." Therefore, Benedick is inclined to believe what they say about Beatrice's love for him. Benedick's complete change of heart about marriage and about Beatrice is obvious in the comparison of his two monologues — before and after his eavesdropping — from his easy talk about the perfection he requires in a woman, to his admission that he "will be horribly in love with her." He recognizes that he is going against his reputation, and others may make fun of him when they find out. But he accepts the fact that he has a right to change his mind:

... doth not the appetite alter? A man loves the meat in his youth, that he cannot endure in his age.

He appears to move toward loving and being loved with relief first and then with eagerness.

When Beatrice suddenly comes to call Benedick to dinner, he interprets even her insults as veiled expressions of affection. She, of course, has not yet been subjected to the planned eavesdrop-ping/noting treatment by her friends (which will take place in the next scene).

ACT III — SCENE 1

Summary

Hero and her two attendants, Ursula and Margaret, plan how they will trick Beatrice into hearing that Benedick is in love with her. Margaret goes to tell Beatrice that Hero and Ursula are in the orchard talking about her and to suggest that Beatrice hide herself nearby to hear their conversation.

When Beatrice has hidden, Hero and Ursula talk about how Benedick is overcome with love for Beatrice. Hero says that Don Pedro and Claudio want her to tell Beatrice about his passion, but she feels instead that he must keep it hidden for fear of Beatrice's ridicule and disdain. Instead, Hero says that she must convince

Benedick to fight against his love. She and Ursula talk about Benedick's many good qualities and his excellent reputation.

When Hero and Ursula leave, Beatrice emerges from her hiding place, astonished at what she has overheard. She realizes that she must change her ways: She will return Benedick's love and express kindness instead of contempt and pride.

Commentary

Beatrice seems surprised that she has such a strong reputation for pride and disdain, and for being self-centered and unapproachable. Just as Benedick did in the last scene, she completely reverses her negative view of marriage. And just as with Benedick, she was always much closer to loving him than she would ever acknowledge. Now she is pleased with the prospect of marrying Benedick, revealing how her deeper feelings differ from the way she appears to others. She admits to herself that she has known Benedick's good qualities all along, in spite of what she has said to him and to others about him, which parallels Benedick's sudden realization that Beatrice possesses the very qualities he insisted a future wife should have.

Quiet, traditional Hero apparently finds pleasure here in criticizing her cousin within her hearing, probably in a rare opportunity to tease her. She may not have the courage to criticize her face to face. They have been best friends and indeed bedmates until now. Hero may wonder how Beatrice will get along without her once Hero is married (and this pretense is an opportunity to send happiness in Beatrice's direction).

ACT III — SCENE 2

Summary

On the day before the wedding, Don Pedro announces to Leonato, Benedick, and Claudio that he will be leaving after the marriage of Hero and Claudio, taking Benedick with him. Benedick admits to the others that he is a changed man, and the other men — all in on the plot to match him up with Beatrice — tease him about his sad expression and his newly shaven face, clear signs that he is in love. He asks to speak to Leonato privately, and they leave. Claudio comments to Don Pedro that Beatrice has by now overheard the contrived conversation between Hero and Margaret.

Don John enters and asks to speak to his brother, suggesting Claudio will want to hear what he is reporting. He tells them that Hero is "disloyal" to Claudio, letting herself be disgraced by another man. Claudio cannot believe this report, and Don John asks that they meet him at night so he can show them what is taking place in Hero's room, even this night before the wedding. Claudio vows to shame Hero publicly if in fact she is guilty of such misdeeds.

Commentary

In this scene, Don Pedro's plot to bring Beatrice and Benedick together overlaps with Don John's plot to disrupt the marriage of Claudio and Hero. Benedick has begun to recognize his love for Beatrice and has taken some tangible actions — like shaving off his beard that Beatrice does not like — to further the relationship. He may be taking Leonato, as Beatrice's nearest of kin, aside to ask his permission to marry Beatrice. Don John takes the next step in his deception first by accusing Hero of infidelity and then by offering to prove it to Don Pedro and Claudio by letting them "note" her treachery that very night. He uses a cruel sarcasm in his accusation of Hero: "Leonato's Hero, your Hero, every man's Hero."

This moment is the second time Claudio has done an about-face on Hero's loyalty based on Don John's information: First, at the dance, he believed that Hero agreed to marry Don Pedro because Don John said so; now he is ready to believe Don John again and, of course, will be convinced when he sees the window scene Don John and Borachio have arranged.

Although Don Pedro was invited to remain at Messina for at least a month, he announces that he will leave for Aragon after the wedding of Claudio and Hero. He may feel that he and his men will be in the way of the newlyweds, or perhaps he never intended to stay too long. He suggests that Benedick accompany him since Benedick has no apparent reason to stay — probably a test of whether his plot to bring Benedick and Beatrice together is having any effect. Benedick immediately shows signs of his change of heart toward Beatrice, but he becomes impatient with the teasing by his friends and leaves to talk with Leonato.

Before Claudio even sees what he thinks is a faithless Hero, he threatens a public humiliation of her at the impending wedding. The audience might wonder why he would do so publicly, reflecting poorly on himself in the process — he is being cuckolded — as well as on Hero. Why not just walk out or write her a note? But no, a public confrontation is what the immature Claudio chooses — resulting in a much better story than if he just walked away.

ACT III — SCENE 3

Summary

Dogberry appears with his deputy, Verges, and the men who will take the night watch "the Prince's watch." Dogberry gives his men their charge for the evening and then leaves them to their duty.

Borachio and Conrade appear and converse, unknowingly within eavesdropping range of the watchmen. Borachio tells Conrade of his romancing of Margaret dressed as Hero in sight of Claudio and Don Pedro and of the considerable reward Don John has promised him for this deception. The watchmen arrest the two men.

Commentary

In Shakespeare's time, officials such as Dogberry and his watch were often depicted as incompetent, and Dogberry is surely one of the most incompetent. Dogberry often thinks of one word but says another, suggesting he uses words beyond his true vocabulary in an effort to sound authoritative and educated. As a result, he sometimes says the opposite of what he means. For example, in his charge to the watch he says, "who think you the most desartless man to be constable?" but he means "deserving" not "desartless" (in some editions, the word is "desertless"). And he compliments Seacoal as "the most senseless and fit man for the constable of the watch" — "sensible"? The watch "shall comprehend all vagrom men" — certainly he means "apprehend all vagrant men." Verges occasionally does the same thing: In his first comment, he suggests as a punishment "they should suffer salvation body and soul" — surely meaning "suffer damnation." (In Act IV, Scene 2, Dogberry makes a similar word switch after hearing testimony from Borachio: "Thou wilt be condemned into everlasting redemption for this.")

Dogberry expresses a unique philosophy of maintaining security: Let sleeping drunks lie, don't make noise, don't meddle with thieves, don't awaken nurses to quiet crying children, offend no one, sleep when you can.

In the 1993 film of the play, Michael Keaton portrays Dogberry as an object of ridicule, entering and exiting with Verges as if they were riding horses. And yet, is Dogberry really as incompetent and fuzzy-headed as he appears on first sight and hearing? Some of his lines have an undercurrent of good sense and wry humor shining through his loose tongue — for example, in his comments on the possible vanity associated with Seacoal's ability to read and write; in the avoidance of argument and violence; and in the metaphor of the ewe, its lamb, and a calf. Perhaps Dogberry is more sly than inept.

The play's audience gets only Borachio's brief description of the crucial love scene in Hero's window. Margaret, who seems quite fond of her mistress, probably does not know what she was participating in, but why does she dress in Hero's clothes and let Borachio call her Hero? (In the 1993 film, the audience sees the erotic Borachio/Margaret scene in Hero's window, while Don John watches from below with Claudio and Don Pedro.)

In Act II, Scene 1, the wedding was set for exactly a week ("a just seven-night") after Claudio proposed to Hero. This present scene takes place the night before the wedding. The intervening days have certainly flown by, most of them apparently uneventful except for the eavesdropping scenes. Shakespeare does not indicate how Beatrice and Benedick behave publicly in each other's presence after their eavesdropping episodes, nor if there are any other efforts to bring Beatrice and Benedick together.

ACT III — SCENE 4

Summary

Early on the wedding morning, Hero and her gentlewomen are preparing Hero for her wedding. Hero sends Ursula to bring Beatrice. Margaret is critical of what Hero has chosen to wear but quickly backs off when Hero scolds her lightly. Margaret also teases Hero about Claudio and his soon-to-be presence in her bed.

When Beatrice arrives, she says that she is not feeling well. Margaret teases her that she is sick with love. Ursula returns to tell them that the men have come to take Hero to the church.

Commentary

Notice the parallels between Beatrice's illness, whatever it is, and Benedick's "tooth-ache" in Act III, Scene 2, and between the teasing of Beatrice by Hero and Margaret here and the teasing of Benedick by his friends in the earlier scene. Both Beatrice and Benedick are suffering through this important change in their mindsets.

Remember that Margaret has participated in the love scene in Hero's window the night before, dressed in Hero's clothes. Perhaps this makes her edgy, so that she argues a bit with Hero about the choice of wedding clothes. Her conversation with Hero has sexual connotations (the quips about the weight of a man), and her conversation with Beatrice has uncharacteristic bite to it as she teases Beatrice about Benedick. Her words and actions suggest that she is unaware that her encounter with Borachio was designed to destroy Hero's reputation — even unaware that they were observed.

Carduus benedictus was the Latin name for Holy Thistle, a popular general remedy of the day, especially for problems associated with the heart. As Margaret intended, the Latin name reminds Beatrice about Benedick: *"Benedictus, why benedictus? You have some moral in this benedictus."* Though Margaret denies the connection, she goes on to talk about Beatrice being in love. This line is a good example of Shakespeare's use of language and ideas of the time, which is likely to be partly missed by today's readers or playgoers unfamiliar with *carduus benedictus* and its use.

ACT III — SCENE 5

Summary

Dogberry and Verges stop Leonato on his way to the wedding. They want to tell him about the two men they have arrested — Borachio and Conrade — and ask him to hold a hearing for their testimony. Dogberry is so long-winded that Leonato becomes impatient and tells them to take statements from the prisoners and bring them to him after the wedding. Dogberry and Verges prepare to question the prisoners at the jail.

Commentary

Dogberry's belabored, convoluted way of speaking serves a dramatic purpose by so confusing Leonato that relating the information that Dogberry's men have — that a fraud has been carried out in the window scene — is postponed, allowing Don John's plot to go ahead. Consider what might have happened if Leonato, on his way to the wedding, had taken time to hear the testimony about the plot to dishonor Hero.

Notice again some of the clever (if jumbled) expressions used by Dogberry: a play on the word "marry," use of the Spanish word "palabras," and the philosophical digression beginning with "A good old man, sir." One of the most outrageous "Dogberryisms" of this scene relates to Leonato's impatient comment that Dogberry and Verges are being "tedious," which Dogberry interprets as a great compliment and then graciously returns the compliment, enhanced. Another gem of Dogberryism is his report of his men's proud action: They have *comprehended* two *auspicious* persons!

ACT IV — SCENE 1

Summary

Leonato suggests that Friar Francis use a short wedding ceremony to marry Claudio and Hero. In answer to the friar's first question, "You come . . . to marry this lady?" Claudio answers "No." Leonato assumes Claudio is joking and explains that the Friar is *marrying* them, that Claudio is *being married to* Hero.

The friar proceeds and soon comes to the question about knowing any "impediment why you should not be conjoined." Claudio challenges Hero, Leonato nervously tries to move the ceremony along, but Claudio chooses to delay further, finally denouncing Hero as a "rotten orange," blushing with guilt, a "wanton," "more intemperate than . . . Venus" or animals that "rage in savage sensuality." Don Pedro joins the condemnation, calling her a "common stale" (a whore). Claudio asks Hero who appeared with her in her window last night, and she denies any such appearance. Don Pedro reports that he, Claudio, and Don John all saw her there. Hero faints, and the three accusers leave.

Surprisingly, Leonato immediately accepts the lies and wishes both himself and Hero dead. He rages against her while Beatrice maintains that Hero is innocent. Benedick wants to believe Beatrice. The friar also speaks up for Hero's innocence, suspects that Don Pedro and Claudio are mistaken, and proposes that they hide Hero away and pretend that she is dead from the shock of the accusation while they try to find out what has really happened. Benedick believes that Don John is somehow at the bottom of the false accusation rather than Claudio or Don Pedro. Everyone agrees to carry out this new deception, hoping that Claudio will realize what he has done and return to grieve over her.

Beatrice and Benedick are left alone. Benedick seems as sure of Hero's innocence as Beatrice is. At last they proclaim their love for one another. Benedick then asks how to prove his love for Beatrice, and she asks him to kill Claudio. After his initial protests that he cannot kill his friend, he finally agrees to challenge Claudio for the sake of Beatrice's love.

Commentary

This pivotal scene contains two contrasting dramatic moments, both of which are climactic turning points in the plot: the denunciation of Hero by Claudio and Don Pedro, which leads to Claudio's abandonment of Hero — a moment of great sorrow for all but Don John; and the admission by both Beatrice and Benedick of their love for each other — a moment of great joy under other circumstances. Following the false denunciation, however, the accusation serves primarily to force Benedick to prove his love by carrying out Beatrice's demand that he challenge and perhaps kill Claudio.

Margaret is not present at the wedding although we would expect her to attend her mistress at the wedding. Because she does not hear the question about who was in the window the preceding night, Margaret cannot protest the accusation against her mistress, admitting it was she, Margaret, at the window with Borachio.

Almost every character in the play reacts in a significant, character-defining manner to the denunciation of Hero — some predictably, some quite surprising:

Hero has her most dramatic moments of the play in this scene but is still quite subdued in her reactions, including a ladylike faint.

As we knew from a preceding scene, *Claudio* and *Don Pedro* are prepared to denounce Hero, believing they have seen her infidelity with their own eyes. Although Claudio's vehemence is a little surprising, the behavior of Claudio and Don Pedro at the wedding is predictable.

Don John twists the blade a little further in his pleasure at how well his conniving has worked.

Don Pedro only serves to back up Claudio, never suspecting his brother's sudden loyalty and support. He seems a weaker man for having been so readily taken in by his brother.

Leonato demonstrates how susceptible he is to the opinions of others. He is so eager to have the wedding take place that he first asks for a short ceremony; later he tries to hasten the wedding along by putting words in the mouths of both Claudio and the friar. After Claudio's angry name-calling of Hero, Leonato immediately accepts the accusations about his own daughter and wishes her dead for her disgrace, demonstrating how quickly he ignores all his history as Hero's father to accept the word of a young nobleman. Soon the fickle Leonato changes again, agreeing to follow the friar's scheme to hide Hero and hold Claudio responsible for her "death." Leonato's own words seem to characterize his behavior: ". . . the smallest twine may lead me."

Friar Francis emerges from being a necessary but insignificant character in the play, to being the voice of reason that changes the course of events with his plan for uncovering the truth.

Beatrice emerges as the strongest character of all. Never does she doubt her cousin's innocence. Even in the moment of acknowledging her love for Benedick, her first thought is for justice for Hero — by killing Claudio, the accuser. In the midst of her fury about Hero, it is easy to miss the ardor of her confession of love for Benedick:

Beatrice: I was about to protest [insist] I love you.
Benedick: And do it with all thy heart.
Beatrice: I love you with so much of my heart that none is left to protest.

Benedick is torn between his loyalties: He wants to support Beatrice, but he is loyal to his friends Claudio and Don Pedro, knowing they cannot have made this accusation without good reason. Thus, he is the first to suggest that "John the Bastard" is somehow behind this false accusation. Then, in the scene alone with Beatrice, he hardly knows how to console her and yet protect his friends. He lets his love lead the way, beginning with his ardent declaration: "I do love nothing in the world so well as you." Although he balks at killing Claudio outright at Beatrice's suggestion, he promises to challenge him and bring him to account. Just as the role of Beatrice meets its emotional peak in this scene, so does the role of Benedick, who must reflect conflicting loyalties and affections in a man who has been openly disdainful of relationships and love.

ACT IV — SCENE 2

Summary

Dogberry, his men, and the sexton prepare to examine the prisoners Borachio and Conrade about their crime. The bumbling questioning by Dogberry first brings denials that Borachio and Conrade are "false knaves." The sexton asks that the witnesses be called to give their testimony on what they heard. George Seacoal, the watchman, gives his evidence, reporting Borachio's overheard statement to Conrade that Don John was a villain who had bribed him to accuse Hero falsely. Borachio does not deny this.

The sexton tells all of them that Don John has secretly gone away and that Hero has died. He instructs that the prisoners be brought to Leonato for judgment, and Conrade makes one final attempt to insult Dogberry, calling him "an ass," to which Dogberry takes great offense.

Commentary

This brief scene makes Don John's treachery public, despite the clumsy examination by Dogberry and Verges. The prisoners first deny any wrongdoing when questioned by Dogberry, but after the specific evidence of watchman George Seacoal, their silence seems to be an admission of guilt. Conrade reacts with one final insult, to which Dogberry responds at some length, disappointed that the insult was not written into the testimony: "Oh, that I had been writ down an ass!"

One sign of Shakespeare's genius is his treatment of many secondary characters. Less skilled playwrights tend to give depth of character only to the primary characters, using the secondary characters to move the plot forward in some way, but without distinction among those secondary roles. Even with the relatively brief appearances of Borachio and Conrade, we catch glimpses of significant differences between their personalities and attitudes. Until this scene, Borachio appeared to be the more villainous of Don John's men: He first eavesdropped on Don Pedro and Claudio; he later proposed the window scene with Margaret; he relished his accomplishment to Conrade in the scene in which they were themselves overheard (note all the "noting" here). But when he learns of the disappearance of Don John (probably with his promised reward for the window scene) and of Hero's apparent death, he seems more subdued, not joining Conrade in the final insult of Dogberry. Furthermore, in the next scene, Borachio freely confesses and, in fact, regrets his actions, expects punishment, and exonerates Margaret.

In earlier scenes, we have seen differences between the personalities and attitudes of Ursula and Margaret. Even the men of the watch were shown to be different from one another in their first scene (Act III, Scene 3). In the present scene, their straightforward reports of few words solve the crime — in sharp contrast to the reports given by Dogberry and Verges. Ironically, the play's resolution rests on the testimony of two minor characters who have little to say — at least competently.

ACT V — SCENE 1

Summary

While his brother Antonio tries to console him, Leonato grieves at the villainy that has ruined his daughter's reputation. When Claudio and Don Pedro appear, trying to leave Leonato's estate, Leonato accuses Claudio of falsely denouncing Hero and, thus, of having caused her death. He challenges Claudio to a duel in spite of their difference in age and their differing abilities with the sword. Antonio heatedly backs Leonato up. Don Pedro maintains that the accusation against Hero was true, and Leonato and Antonio leave them in disgust.

Benedick arrives, and Claudio and Don Pedro tell him about the foolhardy challenge by Leonato and Antonio. Benedick ignores their lighthearted talk. They try to engage his humor by talking about Beatrice, but he continues to ignore their chatter. He then accuses Claudio of having killed Hero by his humiliation of her and challenges him to a duel. He tells Don Pedro that he will no longer be a member of his company and that Don John has run away. Benedick repeats his challenge to Claudio and leaves. They are disconcerted by Benedick's words and his challenge.

Just then, Dogberry and Verges bring in their prisoners in preparation for meeting with Leonato as governor and judge. Don Pedro, recognizing his brother's followers, tries to find out from Dogberry what Borachio and Conrade have done wrong. Borachio himself, with expressions of regret and shame, finally explains Don John's plot against the marriage of Hero and Claudio, and admits it was Margaret and himself in the window — not Hero and another lover. Don Pedro and Claudio are stunned at this news, realizing that Hero was innocent and therefore falsely accused by them.

Leonato and Antonio appear with the sexton. Leonato first confronts Borachio, who readily admits his wrongdoing. Leonato then confronts Claudio and Don Pedro, accusing them of having caused Hero's death. He commands them to tell everyone in Messina that she was falsely denounced and demands that they appear at her tomb that very night. Claudio is to hang an epitaph upon the tomb, singing it "to her bones." Claudio agrees to marry Antonio's daughter the next day, although he has never heard of nor seen her before.

Leonato has one more task to undertake — to find Margaret and find out if she knew she was participating in this horrible plot. Borachio defends Margaret, saying she did not know she was doing anything wrong.

Dogberry makes a final complaint to Leonato about Conrade's calling him an ass. Leonato thanks him for his efforts and asks him to leave the prisoners with him so they can confront Margaret. Dogberry and Verges leave.

Claudio promises to mourn at Hero's tomb that night, and he and Don Pedro leave. Leonato leads the prisoners away to talk with Margaret.

Commentary

Several plot threads are brought together in this scene of frequent arrivals and departures. The several parts of the scene are even more complex when we remember that each person's words and actions are based on differing knowledge of the facts.

At the beginning of the scene, Leonato and Antonio do not know about Don John's plot, but they are certain that Claudio and Don Pedro falsely accused Hero and that her reputation is forever ruined. They know she is not dead but are prepared to say that she is.

When Claudio and Don Pedro appear, they still think that they saw Hero being unfaithful and she was therefore justly accused. They are surprised to learn of her "death" but don't see it as their fault.

When Benedick arrives, he does not know the details of the plot but feels sure Claudio and Don Pedro were set up by Don John. He also pretends that Hero is dead. He doesn't see any humor in his friends' jokes and comments.

When Dogberry and Verges arrive, they know (in their unique way) about the plot set up by Don John, and they know that Borachio carried it out. They think Hero is dead, having been so informed by the sexton during the examination of the prisoners.

When Borachio confesses his part in the scene with Margaret, Claudio and Don Pedro are now fully informed about the plot but still think Hero dead, as does Borachio. Notice that Borachio puts all the blame on Don John, although Borachio himself suggested the window scene.

When Leonato and Antonio return, they too learn the details of Don John's plot and are the only ones with full knowledge of all the facts, including, of course, their own deception about Hero's death, Claudio's grieving, and Claudio's immediate acceptance of Antonio's daughter in marriage. Consistent with his gullibility and quick changes of heart, Claudio rationalizes his denunciation, saying he "sinned not" but made a mistake.

Dogberry's statement of the misdeeds by Borachio and Conrade is a masterpiece of unintentional redundancy: They have "committed false report," "spoken untruths," slandered, "belied a lady," "verified unjust things," and behaved as "lying knaves." Notice too the sequence of Dogberry's enumeration of these offenses: "secondarily," "sixth and lastly," "thirdly," and "to conclude." Then note how Don Pedro mocks him: "First," "thirdly," "sixth and lastly," and "to conclude." Claudio points out that the accusations all boil down to one offense.

Dogberry is still smarting from Conrade's insult in the preceding scene, calling him "an ass." After Borachio's confession to Claudio and Don Pedro, Dogberry reminds them of the insult. Later, he tells Leonato of the insult and asks that "it be remembered in his [Conrade's] punishment."

When Margaret participated in the window scene, it was never clear why she would deceive her mistress. In this scene, Borachio graciously clears Margaret for her part in the scene (is he sincerely in love with Margaret?), although Leonato still wishes to confront her about it.

ACT V — SCENE 2

Summary

Benedick asks Margaret to find Beatrice for him, and they exchange quips that have sexual overtones. Left alone, Benedick tries the song he has written for Beatrice, admitting that writing poetry is really beyond him.

Beatrice comes to him, curious about his challenge to Claudio. He says he is waiting for Claudio's response and quickly changes the conversation, asking her which of his "bad parts" she first fell in love with. She answers "for them all together" and asks him which "good parts" of her he first loved. They continue in this playful conversation until Ursula arrives, summoning Beatrice to her uncle. She tells them about Don John's plot, which misled both Don Pedro and Claudio. Benedick goes with them.

Commentary

Margaret again shows herself to be a young woman with outspoken sexual attitudes, consistent with earlier exchanges with Hero and with Beatrice, and consistent with her unintentional involvement in Borachio's deception. We don't know whether Leonato has talked with her yet as a result of the preceding scene.

Beatrice and Benedick resume their earlier style of playful banter, simultaneously admitting and denying their love. Notice the difference in their use of the pronoun you/thou: Benedick now addresses her with the more intimate "thee" and "thou," while Beatrice remains slightly more remote with "you." Her responses to Benedick's openness about love are still guarded and tentative, probably because she has been hurt by him before and doesn't know whether his love is genuine this time.

Beatrice and Benedick finally learn that Don John was at the root of the denunciation of Hero, letting Borachio set up the window scene with Margaret. So Benedick confirms his initial reaction, and Beatrice must recognize that Benedick was right in his defense of Claudio and Don Pedro. Recognizing how Claudio and Don Pedro have been tricked may help her accept Claudio as a future kinsman in marriage.

ACT V — SCENE 3

Summary

The scene takes place just before dawn at Leonato's family tomb, where Claudio and Don Pedro are to demonstrate their grief for Hero, whom they suppose dead. First, a verse that Claudio has written is read aloud and hung on the tomb. The reading is followed by a song of mourning. As dawn breaks, Claudio and Don Pedro return to the villa to change clothes for Claudio's approaching marriage, presumably to Antonio's daughter.

Commentary

Editions of Shakespeare differ about who reads Claudio's epitaph and who sings the song. For example, in the Oxford University Press edition, Claudio reads the poem and Balthasar sings the song; in the Cambridge University Press edition, an unnamed lord reads and sings both.

The scene provides an emotional contrast with the Beatrice/Benedick scene that precedes it and with the joyous scene that follows it.

ACT V — SCENE 4

Summary

The play's final scene begins with the friar's reminder to everyone — Leonato, Margaret, Ursula, Antonio, Hero, Beatrice, and Benedick — that he never doubted Hero's innocence. Leonato excuses the actions of Claudio and Don Pedro and then reviews what is to happen next in the final deception they have planned. The ladies leave to cover their faces with veils.

After confirming Leonato's approval, Benedick asks the friar to perform a marriage between himself and Beatrice.

Claudio and Don Pedro appear, and Claudio prepares to marry "Antonio's daughter," as he promised. The veiled women enter with Antonio. As soon as Claudio vows publicly to marry this stranger, Hero reveals her identity to the amazement of Claudio and Don Pedro. Once again Claudio is overcome with love for Hero.

Meanwhile, Benedick asks which of the veiled ladies is Beatrice and asks if she loves him. Their usual denials and quick repartee continue until Claudio and Hero each produces love poems Beatrice and Benedick have written to one another. Finally, they happily accept each other. At Benedick's suggestion, dancing begins even before the marriage ceremony.

A messenger interrupts the festivities with the news that Don John has been taken prisoner and is being brought back to Messina. Benedick suggests that they think about Don John tomorrow, when Benedick will invent appropriate punishments for him.

Commentary

In the recap of what has happened, Leonato notes Margaret's part in Don John's plot — to her face, since she is on stage but silent — but he seems to forgive her because she apparently did it against her will. Also, Benedick admits he is glad that he doesn't have to duel with Claudio after all.

True to the pattern they have established, Beatrice and Benedick cannot have a straightforward conversation, even in the middle of Benedick's proposal of marriage. Benedick has obviously abandoned his Act II pledge: "I would not marry her, though she were endowed with all that Adam had left him before he transgressed."

Consistent with his prior behavior, Claudio readily adapts himself, first to a marriage arranged as a form of penance for his part in the denunciation of Hero. (Remember that this new woman is now sole heir to the estates of both Leonato and Antonio.) Then just as readily, he reaccepts Hero as his bride-to-be when she can keep the secret of her "death" no longer.

That both Claudio and Hero just happen to have in their wedding clothes handwritten verses written by Beatrice and Benedick is quite a coincidence since neither Claudio nor Hero knew that Benedick was planning his proposal to Beatrice. (We can wonder when Claudio had the opportunity to find and borrow Benedick's poem.)

The last-minute entrance of a messenger at the festivities provides convenient closure to the play so that the audience is not left wondering whatever happened to Don John. Note that it is Benedick (rather than Don Pedro or Leonato) who offers to design Don John's "brave punishments." We are left to imagine what those will be.

CHARACTER ANALYSES

BEATRICE

Beatrice is one of the most delightful characters in all of Shakespeare — certainly one of the most talkative and witty. She is likely to touch a responsive chord with many readers and playgoers today in light of current social ideas that encourage greater equality and self-assertiveness for women than has been traditional for women of the Western world. The traditional woman of the Elizabethan period, especially of Beatrice's class, is better represented by her cousin Hero — the naive, chaste, and quiet young woman of whom Beatrice is extremely protective. Beatrice is as cunning and forward as Hero is naive and shy.

Beatrice often interrupts or speaks her mind without concern about decorum. Her first line interrupts the conversation between Leonato and the messenger and is loaded with sarcasm and bitterness. Throughout the play, she is very clever with words, displaying considerable intellectual faculty as well as a natural ability for humor. And her way with words is sharpened when the object of her humor is Benedick.

Beatrice's unexplained bitterness toward Benedick is displayed right from the beginning. Then we begin to realize she has been hurt by him. Still stinging from past experiences with him, now she greets him with scorn, wariness, and anger. Eventually we recognize that desire and affection for him are still buried within her. She has learned to use humor and insults to disguise deeper emotions. Yet, when she overhears Hero describing her faults, she is surprised at how she is perceived by others: "Stand I condemned for pride and scorn so much?" She vows to abandon her habits of contempt and pride, and also to let herself love Benedick openly.

Before Beatrice can express her true feelings to Benedick, she may find it so difficult to change her habits of scorn and insult that she has physical symptoms of discomfort: "I am exceeding ill. . . . I am stuffed. . . . I cannot smell." Finally in a moment of high emotion during which she rages over the deception against Hero, she is also able to tell Benedick that she loves him — first tentatively, then without constraint: "I love you with so much of my heart that none is left to protest." Yet at the end, she must have her last hesitation — joking or not:

Benedick: Do not you love me?
Beatrice: Why no, no more than reason.

And when she finally agrees to marry him, she has her last little gibe on the subject:

Beatrice: I would not deny you. But . . . I yield upon great persuasion, and partly to save your life, for I was told you were in a consumption.

Has Beatrice changed over the week or so of the play's timeline? At the very least, her tongue is not so sharp and belittling; at best, she has let herself love and be loved — a miraculous change in such a strong, independent woman.

HERO

In some respects, Hero is a foil for Beatrice — a character whose presence serves to show off or enhance the qualities of another character. (The term *foil* originated as a piece of shiny metal placed under a precious stone to heighten its luster. One of the best-known literary foils is Dr. Watson in the Sherlock Holmes stories of Sir Arthur Conan Doyle.)

Hero has her own story, of course, representing the formal courtship traditions of the period. In any arrangements about marriage throughout the play, she is generally passive. At its start, she is apparently attracted to Claudio from an earlier visit, yet she accepts Leonato's guidance to accept Don Pedro's proposal at the dance. Then she discovers that Don Pedro is pursuing her only for Claudio, and she is happy to accept Claudio. After being accused of deceit with another man, she denies any wrongdoing and faints at the shock of the denunciation. She "plays dead," then pretends to be a cousin ready to marry Claudio and finally unmasks as a loving Hero again.

But at the end of the play Hero is probably less naive about men. She even speaks up for herself to Claudio after her unveiling: "One Hero died defiled, but I do live, / And surely as I live, I am a maid." Furthermore, she takes time to "steal" Beatrice's poem expressing love for Benedick and gives it to Benedick at a crucial moment, probably cementing the bond between Beatrice and Benedick. A changed Hero? Perhaps a first move toward self-confidence and maturity.

BENEDICK

Benedick is almost a match for Beatrice as a memorable Shakespearean character. His apparent misogyny and unwillingness to make a commitment to a woman are almost stereotypes early in the play. His use of language, especially in his "merry war" with Beatrice, prevents him from being the clichéd male who refuses to commit to a relationship.

Benedick has probably had a lot of experience with women, only one of whom was Beatrice. He vehemently declares his intent to remain a bachelor and disparages Claudio for wanting to marry Hero, "Leonato's short daughter." He restates his disdain of love and marriage in a monologue alone on stage — even more likely to express his true feelings than his teasing comments to a companion he will lose through marriage. Throughout the early scenes, his exchanges with Beatrice create a feeling that he "doth protest too much" — that is, he really harbors at least affection for Beatrice.

It takes the "noting" scene near the arbor, arranged by Don Pedro, for Benedick to admit he may indeed be able to love Beatrice since she loves him so much. His subsequent meetings with Beatrice and with his friends show a marked change in his attitudes and demeanor from the early scenes. He recognizes that he may be opening himself up for ridicule at his reversal of his well-known attitudes, but he sees his opening up as a part of maturing. His support for Beatrice after the denunciation, including his confrontation with Claudio, demonstrates not only his commitment to Beatrice, but also the value he places on justice even at the risk of loyalty. He becomes single-minded about marrying Beatrice, probably speaking to Leonato about her immediately after the confrontation with Claudio and again just before the wedding. His new behavior finally culminates in his public proposal to her, risking not only her refusal and contempt, but also the ridicule of the assembled company.

Has Benedick changed during the week of the play? Most certainly, both in his public and his private attitudes. That a dyed-in-the-wool bachelor is transformed into an eager bridegroom is extraordinary, yet Shakespeare makes it believable, with a little help from Benedick's friends.

CLAUDIO

Claudio is less of a foil for Benedick than Hero is for Beatrice, but Claudio's conventionality, his immaturity, and his compliant behavior contrast sharply with Benedick's independent spirit, his jaded opinions about women, and his sense of humor. The reader/playgoer who loses patience with Claudio is glad to find a stronger, seemingly less pliant figure in Benedick.

Claudio was apparently attracted to Hero on an earlier visit, and on his return is completely captivated by her. He may also be looking longingly at what she stands to inherit as Leonato's only child, and what he could gain by being married to her when she does. He seems oblivious to Benedick's scathing remarks about her and his attitudes about marriage. Then he allows himself to be deceived by Don John, not just once, but twice. Later he realizes his mistake and allows himself to be deceived by Leonato in an effort to re-ingratiate himself to the family for his earlier error in denouncing Hero. Finally, he recovers himself completely to marry the original (but wiser?) Hero. Somehow, he has the presence of mind to have with him Benedick's love poem for Beatrice and to make it public at the right time.

Does Claudio change during the play? Not much, it seems. He is still immature, ready to concede to whatever marriage plan is presented to him, lucky that a forgiving Hero and her family will even accept him.

DON PEDRO

At the beginning of the play, one could imagine that Don Pedro might dominate the play's action. He seems to enjoy being in charge, probably as a carryover from his role as prince and military leader. He not only supports Claudio's bid for Hero's hand, but he offers to help arrange it. When the marriage is arranged — after what he sees as a minor misunderstanding — he's ready to get Benedick's life rearranged with Beatrice.

When Don Pedro is deceived by his brother's presentation of the "window scene" between Borachio and a woman he sees as Hero, he is probably shaken by how readily he had been taken in by an innocent-seeming Hero, even helping Claudio to win her. He does not see through his brother's latest act of treachery, even when it's further denied at the wedding. He tries to make light of the consequences when Hero is reported as dead but again must recognize his own gullibility when he hears of his brother's treachery from the mouth of the guilty Borachio. Never again does Don

Pedro appear as sure of himself as he was at the beginning of the play. Even at the final wedding scene, amidst the general merriment, Benedick notices that "Prince, thou art sad. Get thee a wife, get thee a wife."

Has Don Pedro changed? Perhaps as much as any character has, as a result of recognizing his own vulnerability and his ultimate inability to keep control of events around him.

DON JOHN

By his very position in Don Pedro's household, Don John recognizes that he is a "second-class citizen." When he is unsuccessful at gaining recognition through military battle with his brother, he turns his discontent toward conspiracies to hurt those he envies — his brother and Claudio, for example. When Claudio's wedding is disrupted, he runs away, leaving his coconspirator behind unpaid — perhaps a fatal error. Might he have felt any remorse at hearing that Hero died of her shame? Probably not. Anyway, he has been caught and will return for his punishment, at least partly shaped by Benedick.

Is Don John a changed person? Probably not, but then we wouldn't expect true villains to change, especially in a comedy.

LEONATO

Leonato is at the center of events from beginning to end. After the formal welcome of Don Pedro, we tend to forget that Leonato is the governor of Messina, at least until he is asked to consider the fate of Dogberry's prisoners. Leonato lets himself be guided rather easily by the ideas and opinions of others: First, let Hero marry Don Pedro if he proposes. That not being the case, let her marry Claudio (even push the wedding ceremony along when it begins to lag). When Hero seems to prove promiscuous, believe the accusers (after all, they are noblemen) and threaten Hero. When the friar offers another approach to discovering the real villain, accept it enthusiastically (after all, the church should know). When he meets Don Pedro and Claudio, challenge them. When everything seems resolved, encourage Beatrice to marry Benedick. And finally, when Benedick suggests dancing before the wedding, try to insist on the wedding first, but when that doesn't change Benedick's mind, go along with the dancing. And worry about punishment of the culprits another day.

Is Leonato changed? Not outwardly, although he may have greater faith in his own daughter and less respect for so-called nobles.

DOGBERRY

Dogberry begins by being an object of ridicule and ends up the same way ("You are an ass!"). His men discover the deception by Don John — through their noting — but the deception is finally brought to full exposure in spite of Dogberry's efforts rather than because of them. But his role as comic relief is beautifully designed, leaving the audience wondering whether he is truly as confused and simple-minded as he seems. He is left unchanged by the actions of the play, except for his hurt pride.

CRITICAL ESSAYS

ABOUT THE LANGUAGE AND LITERARY STYLE

It's remarkable to realize that *Much Ado About Nothing* was written four centuries ago in the England of Queen Elizabeth I. Across the Atlantic, the first English colony at Roanoke Island had disappeared several years earlier, and the first permanent English colony at Jamestown was still several years ahead. So, near the end of the fifteenth century, England itself *was* the English-speaking world. The language of the play is the Elizabethan English of its day. Shakespeare's frequent similes, metaphors, allusions, analogies, and other figures of speech are often based on ideas, events, and people familiar to most English playgoers of the time.

Shakespeare's gift for words and phrases and his skill at wordplay are extraordinary, one reason why he is still quoted more frequently than any other writer in the English language. Ironically, these qualities in a man of limited education have often given rise to the theories that Shakespeare did not write Shakespeare.

Humor. Elizabethan audiences were especially fond of certain kinds of humor, especially humor that played on words. In her

1993 book, *The Friendly Shakespeare,* Norrie Epstein identifies four types of Shakespearean humor:

- *Puns*: The epitome of wordplay. A pun may be based on different meanings of the same word (as in "noting") or on different words pronounced the same ("whys" and "wise"; "Londonderry Air" and "London derriere"). An example from Act I, Scene 1:

Messenger: [speaking about Benedick to Beatrice] And a good soldier too, lady.
Beatrice: And a good soldier to a lady, but what is he to a lord?

Many puns must be seen in writing to get the joke.
- *Running gags*: An amusing or derogatory jest that recurs many times, usually with variations. For example, a frequent running gag in Shakespeare is of a *cuckold*: a man whose wife is unfaithful. The word refers to a cuckoo, a bird that lays its eggs in other birds' nests. The cuckold was said to grow horns on his head, invisible to him, obvious to everyone else. Thus, words and symbols suggesting cuckolding include horns, rams, and bulls. In *Much Ado*, the preoccupation with cuckolding begins early in Act I, Scene 1:

Don Pedro: . . . I think this is your daughter?
Leonato: Her mother hath many times told me so.
Benedick: Were you in doubt, sir, that you asked her?
Leonato: Signor Benedick, no, for then you were a child.

This same scene includes three more indirect references by Benedick to cuckolding, suggesting that his attitude toward women and marriage is probably shaped by his preoccupation with being cuckolded.
- *Quibbles*: Wordplays that squeeze as many meanings as possible out of one word or phrase. Pronunciation may be important, just as it is in puns. A conspicuous quibble in *Much Ado* is the banter between Don Pedro and Balthasar about notes and noting/nothing in Act II, Scene 3:

Don Pedro: . . . Do it in notes.
Balthasar: Note this before my notes;
There's not a note of mine that's worth the noting.
Don Pedro: Why, these are very crotchets that he speaks.
Note notes, forsooth, and nothing!

> The use of "crotchets" here is another kind of wordplay within the larger quibble on notes and noting, since the word means quarter notes as well as whimsical ideas. Still another form of quibble is the exaggerated use of a metaphor. For example, when Beatrice learns that Benedick is the close companion to Claudio, she says:

Lord, he will hang upon him like a disease: he is sooner caught than the pestilence, and the taker runs presently mad. God help the noble Claudio, if he hath caught the Benedick. It will cost him a thousand pound ere a be cured.

- *Topical humor*: This kind of humor is the most difficult to decipher without more information about typical knowledge and attitudes of the time. For example, in Act II, Scene 1, Benedick asks Don Pedro to find him a mission that will allow him to escape from Beatrice. In his suggestions he includes:

I will . . . bring you the length of Prester John's foot: fetch you a hair off the Great Cham's beard: do you embassage to the Pygmies.

We must rely on the editor's footnotes on Prester John, Great Cham, and the Pygmies to appreciate this humor fully. However, we understand the gist of it even without knowing what these refer to. On the other hand, some humor is easily missed without such historical information. For example, Beatrice's first line asks about "Signor Mountanto." Footnotes explain that "mountanto" is an upward thrust movement in fencing, which Elizabethan playgoers would understand as a kind of slang for either reaching upward socially beyond his level (social climbing) or sexually thrusting upward. Some actors today pronounce the word as "mount on to," making the sexual reference obvious to today's audiences.

It's not essential that today's playgoer understand the underlying references to every humorous remark because the actors can often make the humor clear from their manner of delivering the lines as well as from the context. The reader of the play, however, has the advantage of the footnotes for a richer understanding of Shakespeare's remarkable wordplay.

Structure and repetition. Shakespeare also excels at other forms of wordplay. For example, Leonato comments on the good news of the messenger in Act I, Scene 1: "How much better is it to weep at joy, than to joy at weeping" — one of those quotable lines of Shakespearean philosophy. In Act II, Scene 3, Benedick has a marvelous monologue illustrating several structural variations of repeated words and phrases: his description of the change in Claudio around the repeated phrase "I have known when" and the symmetry of what he looks for in a woman: ". . . one woman is fair, yet I am well; another is wise, yet I am well; another virtuous, yet I am well" and "rich shall she be, that's certain: wise, or I'll none; virtuous, or I'll never cheapen her; fair, or I'll never look on her; mild, or come not near me; noble, or not I for an angel."

In Dogberry's outrage at being called "an ass" by Conrade, Dogberry has a monologue with wonderful repetitions. The sexton, who was recording the interrogation, has left, so Dogberry regrets, "Oh, that he were here to write me down an ass!" In the middle of his complaint, he raves, "remember that I am an ass, though it not be written down, yet forget not that I am an ass," and he ends with "oh that I had been writ down an ass!" And in his self-justification, he reminds everyone of his good qualities with simple symmetry and repetition of phrase:

I am a wise fellow, and which is more, an officer, and which is more, a householder, and which is more, as pretty a piece of flesh as any is in Messina, and one that knows the law, go to, and a rich fellow enough, go to, and a fellow that hath had losses, and one that hath two gowns, and everything handsome about him.

Verse and prose. Many readers come to Shakespeare with the preconception that the plays are all written in verse, specifically in blank verse of iambic pentameter. In actuality, Shakespeare uses both prose and verse. Most of *Much Ado* is written in prose, and thus the segments in verse stand out on the printed page.

The first occurrence of verse is in the Act I, Scene 1, conversation between Claudio and Don Pedro, the first step of Claudio's wooing of Hero. The second use of verse is in Act II, Scene 1, when Claudio bemoans what he thinks is the loss of Hero to Don Pedro. Verse appears next in Act II, Scene 3, as Claudio, Don Pedro, and Balthasar prepare for the deception of Benedick, who is hiding in the arbor. Even in the denunciation scene at the church, Claudio is inclined to speak in verse, and the rest of the cast follows suit until Beatrice and Benedick are left alone. In all their exchanges, excepting the final one before they marry, Beatrice and Benedick speak in prose.

"Thee" and "you." Another subtlety of Shakespeare's language is easily missed by today's listeners and readers. "You" is the polite form of the second person singular pronoun with strangers, for formal situations, and for general usage. "Thee" and its relatives ("thou," "thy," "thine") may be used between good friends or lovers, between a parent and child, and sometimes in a derogatory way.

In the play, the use of "thee" and "thou" comes more easily to the lips of some characters than to others. For example, in Act I, Scene 1, when Claudio and Benedick are alone together, Claudio readily slips into the familiar form, but Benedick does not. When Don Pedro joins them, he begins using the familiar form, but in speaking to Don Pedro, Claudio now uses the more formal "you" as a term of respect toward his superior officer. Benedick uses "you" for everyone. Only in his most loving words to Beatrice after the denunciation scene in the church and at the end of the play does Benedick slip into "thee" and "thine." Beatrice never succumbs to using the most personal form.

As expressed above, today's *playgoer* need not understand all the subtleties that characterize Shakespeare's rich language. The actors' performances should convey much of the intended meaning of a particular word or phrase. On the other hand, the *reader* who takes time to examine the explanatory notes and to reread lines will appreciate more the vitality of the characters and will experience more of the emotional impact of their words and actions in the play.

ABOUT "NOTHING"

The word "nothing" in the play's title has always been the subject of speculation. No one knows if Shakespeare chose the word "nothing" with the intention of being ambiguous. In Elizabethan common dialect, "nothing" was pronounced much like "noting," thus allowing the word to be a homonym (a sound-alike word) with four totally different meanings:

> *nothing* (as in present parlance): not anything, zero, zilch, *nada*
>
> *nothing:* In Shakespeare's time, "thing" and "nothing" ("nothing") were slang words for referring to a sexual organ; thus phrases with the word "nothing" sometimes had sexual or erotic connotations
>
> *noting:* writing musical notes
>
> *noting:* observing, overhearing, perceiving

Note how many key events in the play reflect the last meaning above — overhearing or observing.

Benedick overhears a conversation that informs him that Beatrice is in love with him (Act II, Scene 3). Beatrice overhears a conversation that informs her that Benedick is in love with her (Act III, Scene 1). The watchmen overhear a conversation in which Borachio tells Conrad about faking the scene at the window of Hero's room (Act III, Scene 3).

Antonio reports (incorrectly) to Leonato about an overheard conversation between Don Pedro and Claudio (Act I, Scene 2). Borachio reports (correctly) the same conversation to Don John, leading him to suggest how to use the information for their own purposes (Act I, Scene 3). Don John places Claudio and Don Pedro where they can overhear the mock love scene at the window of Hero's room (between Scenes 2 and 3 of Act III).

Furthermore, these are not the only instances in which the word or action of "noting" occurs rather pointedly. For example, concerning the wordplay in Act II, Scene 3 ("noting" words highlighted below), note that Don Pedro is encouraging Balthasar to sing again:

Don Pedro: Or if thou wilt hold longer argument,
Do it in **notes**.
Balthasar: **Note** this before my **notes**,
There's not a **note** of mine worth the **noting**.
Don Pedro: Why these are very crotchets that he speaks,
Note, notes, forsooth, and **nothing**.

The last line might be paraphrased as "just sing — no more talk."

Another extended scene involving noting is the dancing sequence in Act II, Scene 1. Most of the characters are masked, allowing them to observe others surreptitiously, themselves hidden (un-notable) behind their masks. In the same scene, the audience itself is allowed to overhear snatches of conversation between pairs of characters not sure about the identity of one another.

All threads of the plot and subplots are intertwined with instances of noting — their planning, their execution, and their consequences. So indeed the story is *Much Ado About Noting.*

INTRODUCTION TO THE 1993 FILM
MUCH ADO ABOUT NOTHING

Watching a good performance of a play brings much to its audience that cannot be experienced by reading the play. For example, the playgoer sees real people with their individual expressions and mannerisms, and in costumes and settings intended to highlight their actions. If the viewer doesn't understand every word or line, the action or expression often conveys the meaning. Live theater has a special power to excite, inspire, and involve the playgoer with the action and characters on the stage.

A well-produced, well-directed, and well-cast film may accomplish most of what occurs in a theater, with the added advantages of closeups, speech amplification, greater variety and realism of settings, and special effects not possible on the stage. A film is not necessarily better than a stage production, but rather a different kind of experience with the same story material.

England's Kenneth Branagh is extensively trained and experienced in the production and performance of Shakespeare's plays on the British stage. With his own special viewpoints and skills, he has brought several of them to film, including *Much Ado About Nothing, Hamlet,* and *King Henry V.*

His 1993 film of *Much Ado About Nothing* is an outstanding adaptation of the play that benefits from his judicious cutting and rearrangement of text, as well as from his casting. He has filmed on location in and around an actual sunny Italian villa of appropriate age and condition, the Villa Vignamaggio in Tuscany. The setting contributes greatly to qualities of timelessness and isolation from the rest of the world, as well as to its visual impact.

Casting. The cast of the film adaptation is headed by Branagh himself as Benedick and Emma Thompson (Branagh's wife at the time) as Beatrice. The princely brothers are played by American actors Denzel Washington (Don Pedro) and Keanu Reaves (Don John), and Claudio is played by Robert Sean Leonard. Michael Keaton takes his portrayal of Dogberry to the very edge of buffoonery, and the credulous Leonato is played effectively by Richard Briers. Other characters are portrayed by actors who seem completely comfortable with Shakespeare's language and lines.

New opening. The film immediately establishes a lighthearted mood in a new opening scene: First, over a black screen, a voice slowly recites the first verse of the song from Act II, Scene 3, "Sigh no more, ladies." During this recitation, the words of the first verse appear phrase by phrase on the screen. As the second verse is being read, the sun-washed villa is seen at a distance from a nearby hill, first in a painting that Leonato is creating, then in its reality. Then the camera pans across a carefree scene of a picnic with residents of the villa lounging in the grass and enjoying Beatrice's recitation of the verses from a small book.

Soon after she finishes the last line, the messenger who opens Act I, Scene 1, rides in on horseback. The light and leisurely quality of this opening is shaded by Beatrice's obvious enjoyment of the song's cynicism about the faithlessness of men (a theme of the play).

Cuts and pacing. The action of the first scene follows the playscript sequence, but with cuts of about half the written text, resulting in a considerably faster pace. During the much-abbreviated scene with the messenger, the relationships between Hero and Claudio and between Beatrice and Benedick are quickly established through facial expressions, gestures, and actions as well as the lines.

At the point in mid-scene when Don Pedro and his men appear in the play, another new scene without dialogue is inserted. This new scene shows the villa's residents hurriedly and boisterously bathing and donning clean clothes, while the arriving soldiers do the same. The play's action resumes with a refreshed Don Pedro and his company formally greeting a similarly renewed Leonato and household. The scene continues apace. Overall, the scene is cut by more than half, and yet the omissions are seamless to any viewer who has not memorized the lines or is not following the script.

Branagh has omitted or cut to the bone several subsequent scenes and their lines, sometimes inserting in their place a visual scene that conveys the incident more dramatically than the words. At other times, he has cut lines and thinned out long speeches to keep the story moving and to eliminate unnecessary details. For example, Act I, Scene 2 — a very short scene between Leonato and his brother — is cut completely, so the viewer is spared Antonio's confused report about Don Pedro and Hero. Instead the viewer is immediately plunged into Scene 3, introducing the dark side of the story with Don John and his two confederates, Borachio and Conrade.

Other major cuts include:

Act II, Scene 1: Almost all the initial ambiguous conversation between Don Pedro and Hero has been cut.

Act II, Scene 3, and Act III, Scene 1: Many of the lines among the "conspirators" as they are setting up the eavesdropping episodes of Beatrice and Benedick have been dropped. Instead, the two scenes are primarily the eavesdropping, moving quickly and smoothly from Benedick's to Beatrice's without pause. These two connected scenes are brought to a close with two joyful images superimposed on one another: Beatrice soaring high on a swing and Benedick jumping around in a fountain, both obviously delighted to learn that they are loved.

Act III, Scene 2: Most of the teasing of Benedick by Don Pedro and Claudio has been cut. Instead, a scene is introduced in which Benedick's friends observe him posing before a mirror to adjust his hair and a scarf.

Act III, Scene 2: In the play, Don John lays the foundation for Hero's apparent promiscuity after the dance by talking with Claudio and Don Pedro. That part of this scene has been cut. Instead, on the wedding eve, a few of those lines are used when Don John leads them to a window where they observe Borachio making love to a woman (Margaret) he calls Hero. The scene is enhanced by Claudio's attempt to scream at the pair, Don John's muffling of Claudio, and another view of the lovemakers, immediately followed by a view of Hero asleep in her bed (obviously not in the same room).

Act III, Scene 4: The scene among the women before the wedding has been dropped.

Act V, Scene 3: The scene at the tomb begins with a nighttime candlelight procession to the tomb. At the tomb, Claudio reads the epitaph to Hero and musicians play and sing the short song. No other lines are included.

Perhaps not surprisingly, Branagh retains most of Benedick's monologues in their entirety.

Changes in sequence. Branagh has resequenced several scenes or parts of scenes to good effect. For example:

In the dance scene of Act II, Scene 1, the overheard snatches of conversation among masked pairs are presented in a different sequence.

The scheme to disgrace Hero with a scene at the window is discussed by Don John and Borachio much later in the film (after Act III, Scene 3, instead of as Act II, Scene 2). This is immediately followed by Don John's revelation to Claudio and Don Pedro (formerly Act III, Scene 2) and the scene at the window (not staged in the play). This complete resequencing and tightening of conversation is quite well done, making the whole deception activity more unified and believable.

Benedick's attempts at poetry and song, originally in Act V, Scene 2, are moved to the morning of the second wedding scene, after the tomb scene (Act V, Scene 3), where it seems most appropriate and is more related to the revelations about poetry in that wedding scene.

None of the cuts and changes in sequence alter the story substantially; instead, they clarify the story line and facilitate its pace.

Enhancements. As noted earlier, film can include visual effects and enhancements to the story not possible on the stage. Several of these have already been identified: for example, the opening view of the villa, the bathing scene, the overlaid scene of Beatrice on the swing and Benedick in the fountain, and the lovemaking scene at the window. Other enhancements of note:

Borachio is seen eavesdropping on Claudio and Don Pedro as they discuss the plan for Don Pedro to talk with Hero about marrying Claudio.

As Don John and his men pass Hero, Leonato, and Beatrice in a hallway — after Don John has made tentative plans to disrupt Claudio's proposal — Don John stops to kiss Hero's hand, a gesture of contempt rather than honor. This is then followed by Beatrice's comments about Don John.

During Benedick's eavesdropping on his friends, he tries clumsily to maneuver a folding chair, which eventually lands him on the ground at the moment when he hears that Beatrice really loves him.

Whenever Dogberry and Verges appear or leave, they gallop absurdly on foot as if they were on horses.

Most of the villa's residents are seen at a huge banquet the evening before the intended wedding. Claudio and Hero are observed in intimate conversation and hand-holding. From that bright scene, the viewer is suddenly taken outdoors where several flashes of lightning burst across a night sky — a fitting transition to the next scene, later that evening, when Don John approaches Claudio and Don Pedro to tell them about Hero's infidelity and to lead them to the window where they can see for themselves. The sequence of visual scenes effectively develops a sense of impending trouble.

Not only does a messenger arrive at the end to announce the capture of Don John, but Don John himself is brought in allowing Benedick to deliver his last line about "devising brave punishments" directly to the prisoner.

The film closes with a boisterous dance of dozens of the villa's residents and guests all around the elaborate grounds and gardens of the villa with the camera moving upward and away leaving the viewer with a beautiful panorama of joyful celebration.

Regardless of the other ways one experiences *Much Ado About Nothing* — on the stage or from a book — one can expect an enriching new experience watching Branagh's film.

REVIEW QUESTIONS AND ESSAY TOPICS

(1) Select the love story that you feel is the play's main plot. Explain why you have chosen it. Describe the main plot completely. Explain the role of the other love story.

(2) List all the "pairs" you can identify in the play — for example, pairs of lovers, pairs of brothers, and pairs of maidservants. For each pair, explain why you think both members of the pair were included and how you think Shakespeare used the pairing to advantage in his development of characters and plot.

(3) Who are the two or three leading characters of the play? Explain why. Who are the secondary characters, and what functions do they serve? What functions are served by the remaining characters?

(4) List all the significant instances of "noting" (eavesdropping, observing, or otherwise taking special notice) in the play. For each instance, express why it was included and what it accomplishes.

(5) Review the emotional highs and lows of the play. Make a list of all scenes and rate each scene on its degree of being high or low. Where a "scene" actually has several subscenes, you may find it necessary to rate subscenes separately. Then plot the highs and lows on a simple chart to illustrate how Shakespeare has used the contrast between highs and lows to "play" with the audience's emotions.

(6) Identify all scenes in which verse is used rather than prose. For each of them, explain what effect the use of verse has, if any. Write your ideas about why verse is used in each of those places.

(7) Citing specific lines and scenes in the play, trace Don John's plots against Claudio and Don Pedro from their earliest beginnings to the culmination of each plot.

(8) To some literary analysts, Claudio and Hero as characters suffer by comparison to Beatrice and Benedick. Consider a version of the play in which Beatrice and Benedick do not appear as characters. Write a summary of the play focused on Claudio and Hero and explain what is more effective or less effective about the resulting play.

(9) Write your version of several background stories that take place before the play begins — for example, the earlier relationship between Beatrice and Benedick; the family conflict and the battle between Don John and Don Pedro; the earlier encounter between Claudio and Hero.

(10) Imagine what will happen in the future for Don Pedro, Don John (including what "brave punishments" Benedick might devise for him), Claudio and Hero, Beatrice and Benedick, Borachio and Margaret, Leonato.

(11) Explain why Margaret participated in the window love scene with Borachio. What did he tell her about it, before or after? What did she tell Leonato when he questioned her later? Describe the events of the play from Margaret's viewpoint.

(12) Consider what might have happened if several events had gone differently — for example, if the watch had not overheard Borachio and Conrade; if Leonato had listened to Dogberry and the prisoners before the wedding; if Hero and Claudio had not produced the poems during Benedick's proposal to Beatrice; if Margaret had attended the wedding.

(13) Read Dogberry's lines carefully to see if you can make a case for his being a very clever man who knew exactly what he was doing all the time. Describe examples of his wisdom and cleverness.

(14) If you were to revise the play, what revisions would you make? What events would you add or take out? How would you change the characters? Write a summary of your revised plot, emphasizing the changes.

SELECTED BIBLIOGRAPHY

Annotated Editions of *Much Ado About Nothing*

The Arden Shakespeare. A.R. Humphreys (Editor). London: Routledge, 1998.

Cambridge School Shakespeare. Mary Berry & Michael Clamp (Editors). Cambridge: Cambridge University Press, 1992.

Signet Classic Shakespeare. David L. Stevenson (Editor). New York: Penguin Books, 1964.

World's Classics Series. Sheldon P. Zitner (Editor). Oxford: Oxford University Press, 1994.

Books About Shakespeare and His Writing

BOYCE, CHARLES. *Shakespeare: The Essential Reference to His Plays, His Poems, His Life, and His Times, and More.* New York: Facts on File, 1990.

BURGESS, ANTHONY. *Shakespeare.* Chicago: Ivan R. Dee Elephant Paperbacks, 1994 (orig. publ. 1970).

CHARNEY, MAURICE. *All of Shakespeare.* New York: Columbia Univ. Press, 1993.

DOYLE, JOHN AND RAY LISCHNER. *Shakespeare For Dummies.* Foster City, California: IDG Books Worldwide, Inc., 1999.

EPSTEIN, NORRIE. *The Friendly Shakespeare.* New York: Penguin Books, 1993.

LEVI, PETER. *The Life and Times of William Shakespeare.* New York: Henry Holt, 1988.

MACDONALD, RONALD R. *William Shakespeare: The Comedies.* New York: Twayne Publishers, 1992.

MATUS, IRVIN LEIGH. *Shakespeare, in Fact.* New York: Continuum Publishing, 1994.

ROSSITER, A. P. "Much Ado About Nothing," in Harold Bloom (Editor), *William Shakespeare: Comedies and Romances.* New York: Chelsea House, 1986.

ROWSE, A. L. *Shakespeare, the Man.* New York: St. Martins Press, 1988 (revised edition).

SCHOENBAUM, SAMUEL. *William Shakespeare: A Compact Documentary Life.* Oxford: Oxford University Press, 1977.

VAUGHAN, JACK A. *Shakespeare's Comedies.* New York: Frederick Ungar, 1980.

WELLS, STANLEY. *Shakespeare: A Life in Drama.* New York: Norton, 1995.

WELLS, STANLEY (editor). *The Cambridge Companion to Shakespeare Studies.* Cambridge: Cambridge University Press, 1986.

WILSON, IAN. *Shakespeare: The Evidence: Unlocking the Mysteries of the Man and His Work.* New York: St. Martin's Press, 1994.

NOTES

NOTES

NOTES

NOTES

NOTES

Made in United States
North Haven, CT
22 May 2023

36853603R00039